Praise for THE **ACTOR'S AUDITION**

"The book is great! A must for any budding, blooming, or blossomed actor." —**Jim Dale**

"Wonderful, unusual, and vitally useful. This is from someone who really knows." —**Beatrice Straight**

"A fascinating eye-opener for me." —**Walter Matthau**

"A very useful and valuable tool for beginning actors to prepare themselves for the very difficult process of auditioning . . . it should serve more-established performers equally well." —**Philip Bosco**

"An invaluable handbook for any auditioning actor who is wondering what 'they' are thinking on the other side of the footlights." **—Alexander Cohen, producer**

"A must for young actors." **—Anne Jackson**

"*The Actor's Audition* has such an excellent insight into the process that actors should run, not walk, to the bookstores." **—Ernie Martin, acting teacher**

"Too bad this book wasn't out thirty years ago." **—Tony Randall**

"An invaluable handbook for everybody involved with the audition process. A masterful piece of work." **—Arthur Cantor, producer**

"An extremely useful guide in understanding audition technique, [this book] enhances one's ability to be both perceptive and fair in the vital and delicate business of talent assessment." **—George C. White, president, Eugene O'Neill Theatre Center**

"A most ambitious and interesting book which has a marketplace for writers and agents. It will probably be around for the next fifty years." **—Irving Lazar, agent**

"This book is a daily tool for life as well as the ever-present audition. It has proven very profitable for me." **—Elizabeth Franz**

"Informative and very helpful. The advice the book offers is practical and easy for any actor to apply." **—Theodore Mann, artistic director, Circle in the Square Theatre**

"The most useful and illuminating guide for young performers on the art of auditioning—I wish it had been there for me when I was beginning." **—Kitty Carlisle Hart**

THE ACTOR'S AUDITION

David Black

Foreword by ELI WALLACH

VINTAGE BOOKS   A Division of Random House, Inc. New York

ISBN 0-679-73228-4

Book design by Jennifer Dossin

Manufactured in the United States of America

For Sophie, Sandor, Jeremy, and all
the rest of us who benefit from
successful auditions

Acknowledgments

This book is the result of teaching young actors over a period of several years. It has been a collaborative effort, and I am grateful to all of my students for having shared their thoughts and experiences with me. Much of the early work was done with students at The New School in New York City, where Lewis Falb, chairman of the Theater Department, encouraged my efforts. For the last several years the principal participants have been students of Susan Grace Cohen at John Strasberg's School, and I have particularly enjoyed working with them.

Harold Prince contributed invaluable suggestions for the chapter on the musical audition, and I deeply appreciate his expertise and enthusiasm.

I am grateful to Michael J. Fine, whose friendship helped make this book possible. William Shust was one of the first members of the acting profession to read the manuscript, and Elizabeth Rose contributed thoughtful questions that made me work harder.

Acknowledgments

My editor, LuAnn Walther, provided creative and professional guidance, and my agent, Diane Cleaver, taught me the value of her profession. Susan Brown contributed skilful copyediting, and Stephen Hulburt gave useful advice when it was needed.

Last, but certainly not least, Anne Rivers lived with me during the conception and birth of this book. During that time she inspired me, and also helped me over the rough periods. She made use of her unusual talents to assist me in making the dream of this book a reality. In addition to all of that, during the writing of the book she became my wife.

Contents

Contents

The actor has all the other arts as handmaids: the poet labors for him, creates his part . . . the scene-painter aids him; the costumes, the lights, the music, all the fascinations of the stage—all subserve the actor's effect: these raise him upon a pedestal; remove them, and what is he?

George Henry Lewes
English drama critic and author
(1817–1878)

Foreword by Eli Wallach

I remember one of my earliest auditions. Joshua Logan, as the director of *South Pacific,* had invited me to read for the role of Luther Billis.

"A musical?" I said. "I can't sing or carry a tune."

"Just read," said Mr. Logan.

I walked onstage and saw Richard Rodgers and Oscar Hammerstein sitting in the darkened auditorium with Logan. With my heart thumping, I simply read.

"That was fine," came a voice from the dark. "Now sing."

"What key?" asked the eager pianist.

I knew that in an emergency an actor must remain cool, calm, and collected, so I decided to improvise. I whispered something to the pianist, put an imaginary coin in an imaginary phone to set a scene for myself, nodded to my now friendly accompanist, and started to sing.

"I'll be down to get you in a taxi, honey. Better be ready by . . ." I sang and hung up my imaginary phone. Then I looked miserably out to find my judges in the dark and said, "I've got butterflies in my stomach. I can't sing!"

"That's all right," came the answer, "we'll get you a real phone next time."

I did not get the job. But Mr. Logan, evidently sensing my pain or admiring my improvisatory ardor, later cast me in *Mr. Roberts,* and as a result, I was happily ensconced at the Alvin Theatre for two years.

Why do I tell this story? Well, if only I had been armed with David Black's *The Actor's Audition,* I think I would have conquered the evils of uncertainty that surround the process of auditioning.

This is more than a how-to book. It is not meant to be a panacea for auditions; rather it is an insightful study, a guide through the maze that takes the aspiring or perspiring actor through monologues, readings, musical auditions, interviews, and callbacks into the wonderful world of landing a part in the theater. David Black has provided a wonderful handbook to enable the actor to solve the mysterious puzzle of the audition.

Thinking back over my many failed auditions, I can only ask, David Black, where were you when I needed you?

Introduction

My interest in the audition process began in the sixties, in the early days of my career as a Broadway producer. I was sitting in the Brooks Atkinson Theater with Julie Harris, my star, and Joshua Logan, my director, auditioning actresses for a play called *Ready When You Are, C.B!* A young woman came out on the stage and gave a reading of a scene from the play that made us all burst into laughter simultaneously. Josh laughed so hard he almost fell out of his seat. I signed the actress to a run-of-the-play contract, and she was never funny again.

She wasn't funny in rehearsals. She wasn't funny in previews. She wasn't funny on stage or off. When the play closed a week after it opened, I asked myself, How did this happen?

Granted, I was a young and inexperienced producer, but Joshua Logan and Julie Harris were already enjoying near-legendary status in the theater. How could veteran talent make such a mistake? And even more to the point, why could the actress I hired never again achieve the level of talent she displayed in her audition? She had no wish to sabotage the production. She wasn't being unfunny on purpose.

This experience was to repeat itself many times through my producing career. I began to realize that something happens when actors audition that causes a different effect on the audition audience than what normally occurs in a theater. What was it? Until I found out, I decided to skip the audition process and hire only established and proven talent.

But that didn't work either. I soon discovered that fame, experience, and success do not necessarily mean that an actor knows what he is doing, or that he feels secure with his proven talent. In my production of *The Aspern Papers*, Maurice Evans invented a speech that he introduced one night toward the end of the play. It made his character into a hero instead of the villain written by Henry James and his adapter, Michael Redgrave. Apparently Maurice was confusing himself with the character and was afraid the audience wouldn't like *him*.

I sent John Gielgud the script of a play called *The Ides of March*, which I hoped to produce, asking him to take the part of Julius Caesar. He replied by letter that he thought it was a beautifully written play, but he didn't think he was capable of playing the part! I flew to London and persuaded him to accompany me to Berlin, where we saw a production of the play in German. Gielgud didn't understand a word of German, but when the leading actor got a standing ovation at the end, Sir John agreed to star in my production.

Backstage with Laurence Olivier, when I complimented him with tears in my eyes on his performance as Uncle Vanya, he looked at me and asked, "Did you really think it was that good?" If great talent has no sense of its impact on an audience, and can't decide what roles to play, how could

I as a young producer cast my shows with any confidence at all without resorting to the nightmare of auditions? On two occasions I was lucky enough to see the stars I wanted in action. I chose Alan King for *The Impossible Years* after watching him as Nathan Detroit in the City Center production of *Guys and Dolls*. As a member of the audience, I found out he could act and sing, along with his talents as a stand-up comedian. After seeing Joel Grey in *Cabaret*, I offered him the lead in *George M!* Most of the time, however, I found myself staring in openmouthed disbelief at the antics of actors auditioning. For one musical, an actress spent several minutes putting flowers all over the stage before beginning her song. Another showed up with her own brass band and her mother.

Meanwhile, I was employing future stars without knowing it. In *Look, We've Come Through!* we paid a young actor the minimum salary of the day. His name was Burt Reynolds. In *George M!* we hired a young Bernadette Peters, and in *Salvation,* an Off Broadway musical, I employed a singer named Bette Midler as a replacement after the show had been running for six months. The musical arranger was Barry Manilow. In *The Natural Look,* Gene Hackman and Brenda Vaccaro worked for minimum salaries. If I had really known what I was doing, I would have stopped producing and started managing all this unknown talent.

After twelve years and eighteen shows, I didn't know much more about auditions than when I started. I had learned one important lesson, however. When it comes to Broadway shows, the director, not the producer, is responsible for artistic content. I decided that if I was going to go through the struggle of raising millions of dollars to find out what the critic for the *New York Times* thought of my show, I wanted to be personally responsible for what was happening on the stage. I began a directing career.

As a director, I found I had even more difficulty with

auditions; now I was actually running them. On one occasion I hired a well-known star after auditioning him in a room, only to discover he couldn't be heard in the theater. A star for a musical read the scenes well enough, but since I was functioning as producer as well as director, I let the authors and choreographer handle the singing and dancing auditions while I was out raising the rest of the money. The result was a musical about a song-and-dance man starring an actor who could neither sing nor dance. I should have auditioned the authors and the choreographer. But how? As a producer, I had often wanted to audition the director, or the script. The more I thought about it, the more I realized the importance of auditions for *everyone* connected with a production.

I began sharing my thoughts on auditioning with actors who were in shows I was producing or directing. We formed groups and held practice auditions. New truths began to emerge. We discovered that to have a successful audition, it is necessary to understand the problems of the *employers* of actors. Out of our work came a technique, and actors began to get jobs with it.

This book is a record of our discoveries. It tells how to make the technique work.

Prologue: The Magic of Auditioning

An actor is a magician. He transports us to another time and place. He makes us believe he is someone else. He makes us care about that person and what happens to him. While we are watching, we forget about ourselves and our own concerns. This is truly a form of magic.

But the actor doesn't accomplish this all by himself. There is a script. There are other actors and a director. There is time to rehearse. There is a set with furniture and props. There are special lighting and makeup and costumes. There are also a theater and an audience.

When the actor wants to get hired, he has to audition. At the audition the ingredients that normally help the actor are missing. In addition, the audition audience is not looking for entertainment. That audience is composed of the actor's prospective employers. Before they can hire him, they must be convinced he can do the job. This means they must have the same experience as the audience in a theater. They must feel themselves transported to another time and place. They must care about the character the actor portrays in his audition. How can this be accomplished?

This book offers a technique for auditioning. The technique is based on understanding the nature of the theater audience's experience and the elements that bring it about, identifying which of those elements is lacking in the audition situation, and then finding a way to compensate for each of the missing ingredients.

The technique gives the actor the ability to make his prospective employers care about what happens to him in his audition. It also enables him to involve his audition audience in the life of the character he is creating, as if they were watching a finished production.

There are four types of auditions: when the actor appears alone with a monologue of his choice, when he reads a scene with another person, when he performs a song with an accompanist, and when he is interviewed and there is no set format. Although the four types of auditions share missing ingredients, such as sets and costumes, each presents a different basic problem. When the actor auditions with a monologue of his choice, he has no other actor with whom to work. When he auditions by reading a scene, he has no chance to become familiar with the script, and he has never met the person with whom he must work. When he sings, there is no one to interact with, and the lyrics of the song represent only part of the dialogue from the scene. When the actor auditions by way of an interview, the script itself is missing. The technique in this book gives the actor a method of compensating for the missing elements in each of these situations, so his audition audience will have the same experience as the audience in a theater.

Although this book is written for the stage actor, the technique works for film and television auditions as well. And it works for all the schools and methods of acting.

In addition, this book presents a method for rehearsing each of the audition situations the actor may face, and, further, suggests how an actor can create opportunities to audition.

To have a successful audition, the actor must transport his prospective employers to the imaginary world he creates, without the usual props. He must be able to perform the magic alone.

The
Monologue

When you audition with a monologue of your choice, divide your appearance into four parts. They are:

1. *Appearing as Yourself*

2. *Becoming Someone Else*

3. *Performing the Monologue*

4. *Taking Your Bow*

1: Appearing As Yourself

The person you are is a thousand times more interesting than the best actor you could ever hope to be.

Konstantin S. Stanislavski
Russian actor, director, teacher, and author
(1863–1938)

The people in the audience at your audition are your prospective employers. They will be hiring *you,* not the character you portray in your monologue. Therefore, at the beginning of your audition, appear as yourself.

The people you are auditioning for are very different
from the usual audience. Most audiences go to the theater
to be entertained. They want to escape from the cares of
everyday life, including their jobs. But the audition *is* the
job of the people for whom you will perform. Furthermore,
they have a lot at stake. If they choose the wrong person,
they will lose time, money, and the opportunity to get
further work themselves.

Who are these people? Usually they are the author, the
director, and the producers. If the show is a musical, the
composer, the book writer, the lyricist, the choreographer,
and the musical director will also be present.

To complicate matters, all these people have to agree on

whom to hire. This will not be easy, because each of them has a problem.

For the author, the problem is having to share decisions on casting with other people. After all, he wrote the play. It's hard enough for him to choose anyone. He created the character from his imagination. Now he has to hire a live actor who will bring his own interpretation to the role. The author is beginning to wish he had written a book.

The director is the one who works with the actors. He feels he knows them better than anyone, but he needs the author for rewrites and the producers for money, so he has to listen to their opinions. These obligations worry him. If the wrong choice is made, he will be blamed and will have difficulty getting hired again.

The producers are paying the author and director and are supplying their own services free. They will only make money if the show is a hit. They are concerned that the author and director may side against them in a disagreement. Moreover, some experienced producers resent sharing decisions with producers who are there just because of their ability to write checks.

This is not a happy group of people. You must get their attention and relax them, so they will be able to concentrate on what you are going to do. Use your entrance to accomplish this.

When a character in a play makes his first entrance, it creates a lasting impression. Everything that follows either adds to or modifies this initial impression. Your audition is a play about you, so make the most of your entrance.

The first time your prospective employers see you is when you come into their sight line. There will be no curtain or special lighting to help. Walk in slowly, with a sense of purpose. If you enter too quickly, it will look like you are nervous and in a hurry to get your appearance over with. If your audition is in a room, do not shake hands. In a theater, the proscenium arch separates the audience from the actors, preserving the illusion that the actors exist in another time and place. If you are in a room, you need to create and maintain the same illusion.

As you enter, decide immediately where the center of the stage or playing area is located. When you have reached it, remain silent for a moment. This is the best way to get the attention of your audition audience.

Your first communication must be as yourself. A simple hello goes a long way.

Your hello should include everyone. If you only look at the author, the director will worry that you will never pay attention to him if he hires you. If you address only the director, the author and producers will feel left out. And so on.

After your hello, introduce yourself. Give your name, even if doing so means repeating it after someone has announced you. There is a difference between your saying your name and someone else's saying it. The repetition will have a dramatic effect.

After giving your name, have something prepared to say. It should be only two or three sentences, and you need to know the exact words you will use. Whatever you say must be original. You might express a humorous thought about your place of birth, or share an experience you had on the subway, or comment on the audition space. The important thing is that it comes from you.

By taking the time to communicate at this point in your audition, you tell your prospective audience that you are confident. You also focus their attention on you and create anticipation for what you will do next.

Another important reason for appearing as yourself is that your prospective employers are not looking just for a talented actor. If they hire you, there will be a long period of rehearsals, rewrites, and previews. Your relationship with your employers will be like a partnership or a marriage. Your prospective employers need to know as much as possible about what you will be like to work with. They need to know if you can work with other actors. They need to know whether you will have a temper tantrum if one of your lines or scenes is cut. They need to know if you are intelligent and imaginative and sensitive to other people. They need to know if you work well under pressure. If you enter the audition already "in character," as the person in your monologue, your audition audience will never find out whether you have any of these qualities. Moreover, your prospective employers have never met you. If you enter as Lady Macbeth, they will think that's your real personality.

Even though you cannot display all your positive qualities immediately by yourself, you can give a sense of your personality and imagination by taking a moment to share something of yourself.

Theater is a collaborative art. You will be creating with other people, usually in difficult circumstances. Your audition is also a difficult circumstance because there is so much at stake for everyone. If you show your prospective employers you have the ability to rise above the difficulty, they will begin to realize you are the kind of person with whom they want to work.

After sharing a moment of yourself with your audition audience, you need to introduce the character you are going to portray in your monologue.

You can say something general about your character, such as "This is from Neil Simon's *Last of the Red-Hot Lovers*. An unhappily married woman has been rejected by a prospective lover." Or you can mention your character specifically, as in "The piece I will perform is from *Mean Streets*. Johnny has just missed a payment to the mob." The information you must communicate is the problem confronting your character. Your audition audience has not spent two hours getting to know your character the way the audience in a theater would. They need to be brought up to date so they can identify immediately with what your character wants. You need to know and rehearse the exact words you will use for this purpose. Your audition is a play about you, and how you introduce the character you will portray is part of the script. If you announce that you will be performing a scene in which "Ruth is talking to her sister Joan about her feelings for her boyfriend Bob," you will not be arousing any interest in what you are about to do. If, on the other hand, you say, "A prostitute is about to get married," you will have created immediate sympathy for your character and interest in what you are about to do.

Sharing information about your character and the situation he finds himself in also allows you to demonstrate another aspect of your acting talent—your ability to analyze a scene and a role.

By communicating with your prospective employers before beginning your monologue, you introduce them to the most important character in your audition: yourself.

2: Becoming Someone Else

We must never shirk the preparation in the wings, the practicing of the old self-hypnotic act to transform ourselves completely before we step onto the stage.

Laurence Olivier
English actor
(1907–1989)

After appearing as yourself, you need to concentrate for a moment before beginning your monologue. When you are about to enter a scene in a play, you usually take a moment to think about what you are going to do. You accomplish this in the wings, or onstage if you are to be discovered there when the curtain goes up. In your audition there is no curtain, and you are already on stage.

In order to concentrate, you need to block out the people with whom you have been communicating. Achieve this by going into a freeze: staring straight ahead, closing your eyes, bowing your head, or turning your back.

While you are concentrating, the people you audition for experience a dramatic moment. This is something a normal theater audience never gets to see—the magical point in time when you become someone else. While you are concentrating on what you are about to do, you are also preparing your prospective employers for their trip to the imaginary world to which you are taking them. And you are creating anticipation, as if the houselights were going down in the theater.

Taking time to think about what you are about to do in front of your prospective employers also shows you can concentrate no matter what the circumstances. This is important because on opening night you and your fellow actors will be onstage with the fate of the production in your hands while your prospective employers will be only nervous spectators. Before they hand over this kind of responsibility to you, they need to know you have what it takes.

Your audition is your opening night. The audition audience has never seen you before. Your ability to use your willpower to concentrate in front of these people tells them you have the necessary stage presence.

During your moment of concentration, think about what happened to your character just before the monologue begins. This is the best way to get into his skin as quickly as possible.

When you come out of your freeze, it will be an exciting moment. Your prospective employers will know you are about to speak as the character.

Appearing as yourself and then concentrating on what you are about to do in your monologue take only about thirty seconds, but this brief period is the most important part of your audition. Without these moments, your audition audience will not be receptive to what you do with your monologue. If you handle this time well, your prospective employers will be interested in you, even if they feel you have chosen the wrong material. Showing your positive qualities and stage presence could persuade them to ask you for a different monologue, or even to offer you a chance to read for the show.

3: Performing the Monologue

> When you find yourself alone on the stage speaking a monologue, you are in reality not alone. You couldn't play the part all by yourself. You are surrounded by the presence of the other actors—your partners—even if they are at this particular moment, not on the stage.
>
> Erwin Piscator
> German director, teacher, and author
> (1893–1966)

When you appear in a play, you use yourself to interpret the role you are performing. By bringing your unique physical presence and life experience to the part, you make the character come alive. Your purpose is to work with the other actors to tell the story of the play.

In your audition, your purpose is to show that you have the skills and tools to practice the craft of acting. You *use the character to show you can act.* This means that the monologue you pick and the way you perform it must convey your acting strengths.

The character you use for your audition should be the kind of role you enjoy doing. Don't try to please the people you audition for by portraying a character you think they want to see. *Your prospective employers don't know what they want.* Their search for the right actor is like falling in love; they won't know what they want until they see it. They won't know it's happened until it happens.

Make the character in your monologue come to life. This

is the only way to show you can act. After you have successfully drawn your audition audience into your imaginary world, they will start to have images of you playing a part in their new production. They might decide to have you read for a role other than the one you thought would be best for you. Would that be so terrible?

The monologue you choose for your audition must show your character *dealing with a conflict* over something in which he has a lot at stake. This allows your audition audience to root for him as if they were watching a character in a finished production. *Do not assume a monologue establishes sympathy just because it appears in a published collection.* Some monologues work only in the context of a play, and they may never allow you to involve your audition audience enough to care about the character you create.

Remember, the audience watching a play gets to know each character over two hours. Your audition audience must become immediately involved with your character. They must know *who is saying what to whom and why.* Sometimes this information is in the monologue itself: "To be or not to be" tells what Hamlet has at stake. "Whether 'tis nobler in the mind to suffer the slings and arrows of outrageous fortune or to take arms against a sea of troubles . . ." explains his conflict. If your monologue does not explain what is happening, you must clarify the situation confronting your character when you appear as yourself.

Your monologue is always spoken to another person. Even Hamlet's soliloquy, in which he is talking to himself, is addressed to someone. When people talk to themselves, they assume someone is listening. In your audition, you must decide where the listener is located. If you are in a theater, place the imaginary person you are talking to downstage with his back to the audience. If you are in a room, put him directly ahead of you and behind your audition audience.

13

Never use a member of your audition audience as your imaginary partner. If you do, he will wonder what he did to deserve your attention. You will destroy the illusion you are working so hard to create. Imagine the people you are auditioning for are sitting in the dark where you cannot see them, just as they would be in a theater.

Establish the location of the imaginary person you are talking to by looking at the spot you have picked at the beginning of your monologue. But do not keep your eyes glued to that spot all the time. When two people are communicating, the one who is talking is involved in the images and emotions of what he is talking about. Return to your point of focus when you want to emphasize something or when you want a response from your imaginary partner.

Before the audience in a theater can start to care what happens to a character, they must feel the actor believes in what he is doing. Your belief in the life you create on stage makes it possible for the audience to accept the play's imaginary circumstances. The audience believes you are living truthfully on the stage when they see you reacting to people, events, and circumstances that block what your character wants. In your audition, you are alone, which means you must find a way to bring the obstacles confronting your character to life, so that you can react to them.

Since your partner is imaginary, plan in advance what his attitude will be at each moment of your monologue, then work out your own reactions. The audience starts to believe an actor when they observe him *listening* to other actors. Take time to observe and listen to your imaginary partner. During these pauses, focus on what your character is trying to achieve and react to what you have decided your imaginary partner is doing or thinking.

To compensate for the lack of another actor to listen to in your audition, create opportunities to react during your monologue. If you have been thinking about what happened to your character the moment before your monologue begins (during your moment of concentration), it will seem as if you are reacting to something your imaginary partner said when you start to speak. Your monologue will appear to be a conversation in progress, and you will breathe immediate life into your character.

Using imaginary physical objects to react to also makes your monologue more vivid. If you slowly pick an imaginary ring up off the floor and examine it before you begin Viola's speech "I left no ring with her . . ." from *Twelfth Night,* you will create a dramatic effect before your first words are spoken.

Give yourself characters to react to by finding or creating monologues in which you quote what other people have said. This approach also gives you a chance to play different roles. In *Does a Tiger Wear a Necktie?* Bickham quotes what his father said when his father showed him a faked dirty picture of himself as a baby.

"How ya like *that* for a kid?" he says. "Takes after his old man, huh?" . . . I *hit* him, and I *hit* him, and I *hit* him.

If your monologue contains an unforeseen event that changes what your character is trying to accomplish, you will have more to react to. In *The Time of Your Life,* Joe is on the phone telling his girlfriend that he can't live without her. Then he discovers he has been pouring his heart out to a wrong number. But the girl at that number seems interested. He ends up making a date with her.

An actor in a play makes his character come alive for the audience by being unpredictable. He keeps people guessing about what he will do next. He pursues his character's objective, but he surprises the audience with his choice of means to obtain his goal. This quality also creates an impression of spontaneity and gives the audience the feeling that what they are witnessing is happening for the first time. The greater the variety of approaches the actor is capable of, the more interesting his character becomes.

Since your purpose in the audition is to show your acting ability, you need to change the ways you pursue your objective as often and as quickly as possible. Because there is no other actor working with you, you cannot wait for a negative response to change your approach. Write one or two words next to each line where you plan to change your tack. These words will become like musical notations that tell you how to perform a song. They will remind you of what you are going to do when you glance at the text before each audition.

Use your imaginary partner as if he were an actor onstage with you. If your goal is to extract an important piece of information, woo him, then threaten him. Tease him, then frighten him. The greater the contrasts between the means you choose, the more quickly your character will come to life. Your audition audience will feel your character's need. They will want him to achieve his goal.

Make your first approach a strong one, to propel yourself into the scene. Don't expect to warm up during your monologue. By the time you do, your few minutes will be over.

Use whatever you do best as an actor to achieve the purpose of your monologue. If sarcasm is one of your acting strengths, and the monologue you are performing comes from the first act of a play in which your character is depressed in the first act and sarcastic in the second, don't wait. Your audition does not have a second act. Use your talent for sarcasm in the monologue.

You are not auditioning to show your knowledge of plays and roles. You are auditioning to show you can act. *If the director stops you and asks you to do the monologue differently, it means you have gained his interest.*

End your monologue *before* your character resolves his conflict. When you are ready to stop, freeze and look directly at your imaginary partner as if waiting for a response. Remain in your pose for at least three seconds. Your audition audience will expect you to continue. When the three seconds are up, indicate you are finished by relaxing and becoming yourself again. Nod your head in a bow with a thank-you. Taking your audition audience by surprise at the end of your monologue leaves them wanting you to continue. Your prospective employers will realize they care about the character you have created, as if they were an audience watching your performance in a theater. They will recognize that you enticed them into your imaginary world. They will know you are capable of performing your job.

4: Taking Your Bow

You've got to pretend to believe, because no one
else will believe you unless you believe it yourself.
Ralph Richardson
English actor
(1902–1983)

When the curtain comes down at the end of a play in a theater, both audience and actor need time to recover from the experience they have just had. The curtain gives them that opportunity. When it rises again, the actor is ready to take his bow as himself, and the audience is ready to release their emotions by applauding the actor. In your audition, your three-second freeze at the end of your monologue takes the place of the curtain's closing.

When you come out of your freeze, the people in your audition audience will feel like applauding, but they won't. The producers will be afraid it will cost them more money if they show their appreciation and end up hiring you. The author will worry that you won't agree to rewrites if he flatters you by applauding. The director will be concerned that you will be harder to direct if he shows he likes you; in addition, he may not want to tip his hand to his colleagues. In other words, at the end of your monologue your audition audience will have returned to being prospective employers. When you take your bow, you feel a release from the concentration you used for your work. Demonstrating that you take that work seriously will make the people you audition for do the same. If you feel dissatisfied with your performance, *don't show it*. You are still on stage, with the power to influence your audience. Only you know you might have done it better. If you look unhappy, or hang your head, or apologize verbally, you will destroy everything you have achieved. Furthermore, you are not the best judge of your own work.

In a play the actor gives life to his character and to each scene by pursuing an objective. He tells the story of the play with the other actors, who are also pursuing their individual goals. There is no way an actor can tell what a member of the audience is feeling at any given moment or with whom he is identifying.

This is also true in your audition. If you have lived truthfully with your imaginary partner while pursuing your objective, you have done all you can to create the magic. There is no way for you to judge the result.

Assume you have been successful. Smile when you say "thank you," as if you were saying "you're welcome." Your enthusiasm for what you have done will communicate itself to your prospective employers just as the emotions you expressed in your monologue did.

After your thank-you, exit the same way you entered; walk out slowly, with dignity and a sense of purpose.

5: Reviewing Your Audition

The talent of the actor, when he has quitted the
stage, exists no longer.

François-Joseph Talma
French actor and author
(1763–1826)

It's depressing to perform for an audience that doesn't respond. Don't waste time thinking about whether they liked
you or not. Use the time after your audition to evaluate your
performance while it's still fresh in your mind.

Go over each of the four parts of your audition sepa-
rately. Were you relaxed when you appeared as yourself?
Did you enjoy what you were doing? Did you feel you were
imposing on the time of your prospective employers? Did
you enter too quickly? Did you speak too fast? Did you feel
confident? Did you enjoy sharing your thoughts? Did you
feel in control of the stage or playing area? Did the fact that
you were prepared make giving a sense of yourself seem
like a performance, or were you able to feel you were behav-
ing spontaneously? Did you feel any resentment or hostility
toward the people you auditioned for? Were you angry at
having been kept waiting? Did any of these negative
thoughts come into your mind? If they did, were you able

to get rid of them by thinking about the needs and problems of your prospective employers?

When you took your moment to concentrate before beginning your monologue, were you able to block out your audition audience and concentrate on what happened in the life of your character just before your monologue? Did you feel pressure to begin, or did you start when you were feeling like the character?

Were you able to react to your imaginary partner with the first line of your monologue? Did you pause to allow time for your reactions? Did you feel you entered the world of the play? Were you successful in using all the ways you had planned to pursue your objective? Did you enjoy playing the character? Did you feel as if you were involved in his life and what he wanted to achieve?

If the director stopped you in the middle of your monologue, did you get angry and ask if you could finish, or did you think about the possibility that he liked you? Once he had made up his mind to call you back for a reading, he may have seen no reason to have you continue. Maybe he couldn't tell you he liked you because he didn't want to tip his hand to the author and producers. He may have been hoping they had come to the same conclusion, so that later he could pretend to go along with it. Maybe he stopped you abruptly just to see how you would react, to get a better idea of what you might be like to work with. Did you handle the moment gracefully? Did you show your belief in your own ability by not taking the interruption personally?

If you got lost in the middle of your monologue, did you apologize and ask if you could start again, thereby calling attention to a mistake your audition audience was not aware of? Or did you make it seem like a spontaneous ending by bowing and saying "Thank you"?

When you took your bow, were you thinking you deserved it? Did you feel as if you were saying "You're welcome" instead of "Thank you"?

Think of your audition as a show you wrote, directed, and starred in. *Only you know if it was a success* because only you know its potential. To improve your audition, you must constantly rehearse it. When you start to relax and enjoy what you are doing, your audition will have reached its full potential. Even though your performance may vary, you will be appearing in a hit. Your prospective employers will feel and share your confidence and enjoyment.

If you never hear from the people you auditioned for, don't jump to conclusions. Maybe you reminded the producer of his ex-wife. Maybe you were too tall for the actor they had already hired to play opposite you. Maybe they couldn't raise the money to produce the play. Maybe the author wrote your part out of the play. If your audition was for a repertory company, perhaps someone on the board of directors decided he didn't like the script. There's no telling what might have happened, and no point spending time speculating.

If you do get called back, you will have to audition again. This time, however, there will be a script and another person with whom to work.

The
Reading

When you audition by reading aloud from a script with an-other person, you have no chance to analyze the play and your role, and no opportunity to memorize the text. You will not have met the partner you are working with, and you have no time to work out what your character is trying to achieve in the scene. You must deal with each of these problems to give your prospective employers the same experience the au-dience in a theater would have.

6: Making Your Contribution

When you audition for a new play by reading a scene, you will not have a chance to prepare the way you did when you auditioned with your monologue. In fact, you may be asked to read the scene cold, without ever having seen it. If that happens, ask if you can have a few minutes to look it over. You may get the time if you ask for it. If your request is denied, it will still remind your prospective employers that you have never seen the words you are about to speak. It will also add to the impression you make with your confidence and willingness to take a chance when you go ahead anyway.

In a reading there is no chance to analyze the script and your role, to decide what your character is trying to achieve in each scene. The director will tell you as little as possible, because he has not worked out these ideas for himself. Moreover he and the author and producers are, in most cases, just getting to know each other. In fact, your reading may be their first experience working together. They will be hesitant to express their ideas in front of you.

In addition to auditioning you and each other, your prospective employers may also be auditioning the script. They don't necessarily know what it sounds like. Does the dialogue ring true when it is delivered by live actors? Is it as funny as it looked on paper?

Plays are brought to life in rehearsal by a collaboration among the director, the actors, and the author. Your contribution is unique during this process because you look at what is happening from the point of view of the character you are playing. Your prospective employers want to see what you can bring to the part. You may have ideas about your character which will make the author want to change some of your dialogue and the director some of his staging.

In your audition they need to find out if you have the intelligence and imagination to make this contribution and if you have the courage to express your ideas. What you bring to the reading will be an indication of whether you have these qualities. You should enjoy this situation. The less you know about the character, the more freedom you have to use your imagination to create him.

For a successful reading—just as for a successful monologue audition—you need to involve your audition audience in *your* story as well as that of your character. Taking a risk with material with which you are not familiar and making maximum use of yourself inspire your prospective employers to identify with you as if they were watching a character they cared about in a play.

7: Using the Script as a Prop

The function of the actor is to make the audience
imagine for the moment that real things are happening to real people.

George Bernard Shaw
British playwright, author, and drama critic
(1856–1950)

If you have a chance to look over the scene you are going
to read, *do not memorize it.* Use the script as a prop during
the reading to remind the people you're auditioning for that
what you are doing is an *improvisation.*

If you memorize the lines, they will expect a finished
performance. In addition, you will spend most of your time
trying to remember what you memorized instead of concentrating on your partner and your goal in the scene. The
effort to remember the lines will limit what you do and take
away from the spontaneity of your reactions to your partner, since you will have memorized inflections and phrasing as well. Moreover, your partner will probably not have
memorized the text, and the scene will lack any chance of
achieving theatrical truth because of this discrepancy.

When it is your turn to speak, look at your first speech
and grab as many words as you can remember; then deliver
them to your partner. *Do not look at the script while you are
talking.* When you run out of words, look back at the script,

even if you are in the middle of a sentence. Grab as many more words as possible, and then deliver *them* to your partner. Looking back at your script will not take away from the reality of what you are doing. *It will add to that reality.* When you search for your lines, it reminds your audition audience that you are not familiar with the script, and this adds to your magical ability to become someone else.

By not looking at the script when you are speaking, you allow yourself to relate what you say to your partner. Likewise, when your partner is speaking, allow yourself to focus your total attention on him. *Do not look at the script to find out what you are supposed to say next.* This is your chance to react to another actor just as you would in a finished production. Your reactions will be based on what he is doing. You won't have to make them up, as you did with your imaginary partner in your monologue. If you are totally involved with what your partner is saying and doing, your character will come to life. But you cannot react to what your partner is doing if you are looking at your script. If he stops, and you are looking at him when it is your turn to speak, it will seem as if you are so caught up in the scene that you forgot to check on what you were supposed to say next.

By never looking at your script when you or your partner talk, you free yourself to act spontaneously, just as you would if you had memorized the script and rehearsed. By using the script as a prop, you remind your audition audience that you don't know the lines and give yourself the chance to relate to the other character as if you were already living in the imaginary circumstances of the play.

8: Treating Your Partner as if You Had Already Rehearsed Together

That which hinders your task *is* your task.

Sanford Meisner

American actor and teacher

(1905–)

When you are appearing in a play, you know what the other actor in the scene will be doing because you have rehearsed with him. When his performance varies, you can react spontaneously because you know what your character wants to achieve in the scene. Watching your partner and knowing your objective allow you to deal truthfully with each moment as it occurs on the stage.

When you audition with a reading, you have not had a chance to work with the person you are appearing with, and you have no way of knowing what he is going to do. He may be another aspiring actor like yourself, or he may have been hired for the day to read with all the actors who are auditioning. He may not be an actor. He may be the stage manager or the stage manager's assistant. He may have no acting experience at all. He may be tired or bored or angry at having to read with you.

To deal truthfully with your partner in these circumstances, treat him as if you had already rehearsed with him.

No matter what he does, *react to him the way your character would,* in light of what you are trying to achieve. Do not show anger or hostility. If you do, your prospective employers will notice and will decide that you do not work well with other actors. Revealing negative emotions will also keep your audition audience from believing you are living truthfully in the imaginary circumstances of the play.

If you are reading a seduction scene and the actress you are supposed to be seducing is not reacting, use her unresponsiveness as a reason to try a different approach. If she reads her reply to your ardent words in a monotone, as if she were falling asleep, pretend the scene was rehearsed that way and become even more seductive.

If you are reading a scene in which your goal is to get your partner to join you in an underhanded scheme, and the actor you are reading with starts yelling his lines for no apparent reason, use a quiet, soothing approach, as if you are telling him he will feel calmer if he joins you.

By treating your partner as if you had already rehearsed with him, you free yourself to concentrate on reacting to what he does as you would in a finished production.

9: Inventing a Goal

The audience comes into the theatre inactive and becomes active only as a result of what the actors do. Therefore, the basic problem for the actor is not how he deals with his material in terms of his audience, but how he begins to make his material alive to himself.

Lee Strasberg
American acting teacher
(1901–1982)

An actor in a play uses himself and his technique to bring his character to life. Without him the character would remain printed words on a page. The actor's purpose is to help tell the story of the play. In each scene in which he appears, the actor has to make a decision about what his character wants. When he knows his character's objective, he can react to what the other actors are doing.

When you audition by reading a scene from a play, you have to bring your character to life in order to show your acting talent, but you cannot tell the story of the play because you don't know what it is. Even if you've had a chance to read the script, you will not have time to discuss an interpretation of your role or the play with the author or director. Since you cannot bring your character to life without knowing his goal, *you* must decide what he is trying to achieve in the scene.

Because no one has told you your character's motivation,

you cannot make a wrong choice. The only mistake you can make is not to have *any* goal.

The audience at a play understands what each character wants. This is what gets people involved and makes them care about what happens to each of the characters. The audience gets their knowledge of what each character wants by getting to know the characters during the performance.

The audience at your audition does not have the time to get to know the characters the way the audience in a theater would. They know the story of the play, but, in the case of a new play, even the author has not made up his mind what each character wants in all the scenes. This is part of the work he will be doing with you and the director during rehearsals. To make your audition audience care about your character in the reading, pick a goal for him to pursue.

The audience at a play believes an actor when they decide that the actor believes in what he is doing. Having a goal is the best way to find theatrical truth quickly. Your audition audience does not have to know what the goal is, but they must sense that you have one.

If you choose an imaginative goal, it will make your character more interesting to your audition audience. The stronger the goal you pick, the more mystery and unpredictability you add to the scene. Your prospective employers will be drawn into your imaginary world and will want to remain there to see what happens next. They will believe in the life of the character you have created.

If you have a chance to look over the scene before you read, you may discover that what your character is trying to achieve is clearly indicated. If there are no obvious clues, *invent* an objective for the scene. If you are reading cold, the first lines you speak may suggest what your character is after. If his intentions are not clear, *improvise* a goal to pursue while you are reading.

Let's consider two examples.

If you are reading for Beth in the second act of Simon Gray's *'Otherwise Engaged'* and you have had a chance to look over the scene, you know that Beth's purpose is to get her husband, Simon, to give his permission for Beth to marry her lover, Ned:

BETH: What did Stephen tell you, please Simon.

SIMON: Nothing. Nothing, except for the odd detail, that I haven't known for a long time. So you see it's all right. Nothing's changed for the worst, though it might if we assume we have to talk about it.

BETH, *long pause:* How long have you known for?

SIMON: Oh—*(sighs)* about ten months it would be roughly. *Pause.* How long has it been going on for?

BETH: For about ten months, it would be. *Pause.* How did you know?

SIMON: There's no point, Beth—

BETH: Yes, there is. Yes, there is. How did you know?

SIMON: Well, frankly, your sudden habit, after years of admirable conversational economy on such day-to-day matters as what you'd done today, of becoming a trifle prolix.

BETH: You mean you knew I was having an affair because I became boring?

SIMON: No, no, overdetailed, that's all, darling. And quite naturally, as you were anxious to account for stretches of time in which you assumed I *would* be interested if I knew how you'd *actually* filled them, if you see, so you sweetly devoted considerable effort and paradoxically imaginative skill to rendering them—for my sake I know—totally uninteresting. My eyes may have been glazed but my heart was touched.

BETH: Thank you. And is that all you had to go on?

SIMON: Well, you have doubled your bath routine. Time was, you took one immediately before going out for the day. These last ten months you've taken one immediately on return too. *Pause.* And once or twice you've addressed me, when in the twilight zone, with an unfamiliar endearment.

BETH: What was it?

SIMON: Foxy. *Little pause.* At least, I took it to be an endearment. Is it?

BETH: Yes. I'm sorry.

SIMON: No, no, it's quite all right.

BETH: You haven't felt it's interfered with your sex life then?

SIMON: On the contrary. *Quite* the contrary. In fact there seems to have been an increased intensity in your—*(gestures)* which I suppose in itself was something of a sign.

BETH: In what way?

SIMON: Well, guilt, would it be? A desire to make up—

BETH, *after a pause:* And did you know it was Ned, too?

SIMON: Ned *too?* Oh, did I also know it was Ned? No, that was the little detail I mentioned Stephen did provide. Ned. There I *was* surprised.

BETH: Why?

SIMON: Oh, I don't know. Perhaps because—well, no offense to Ned, whom I've *always* as you know thought of as a very engaging chap, in his way, no offense to *you* either, come to think of it, I'd just

imagined when you did have an affair it would be
with someone of more—more—

BETH: What?

SIMON: Consequence. *Overt* consequence.

BETH: He's of consequence to me.

SIMON: And *that's* what matters, quite.

BETH: What did you mean, when?

SIMON: Mmmm?

BETH: *When* I had an affair, you said.

SIMON: A grammatical slip, that's all. And since the
hypothesis is now a fact—

BETH: But you used the emphatic form—when I
did have an affair—which implies that you posi-
tively assumed I'd have an affair. didn't you?

SIMON: Well, given your nature, darling, and the
fact that so many people do have them these days,
I can't see any reason for being bouleversé now
that you're having one, even with Ned, can I put
it that way?

BETH: Given what about my nature?

SIMON: It's marvelously responsive—warm, a
warm, responsive nature. And then I realized
once we'd taken the decision not to have chil-
dren—and the fact that you work every day and
therefore meet chaps—and pretty exotic ones too,
from lithe young Spanish counts to experienced
Japanese businessmen—not forgetting old Ned
himself—it was only realistic—

BETH: From boredom, you mean. You know I'm
having an affair because I'm boring, and you assumed I'd have one from boredom. That's why
I'm in love with Ned, is it?

SIMON: I'm absolutely prepared to think of Ned as
a very, very lovable fellow. I'm sure *his* wife loves
him, why shouldn't mine.

BETH: You are being astonishingly hurtful.

SIMON: I don't want to be, I don't want to be! That's why I tried to avoid this conversation, darling.

BETH: You'd like to go back, would you, to where I came in, and pretend that I'd simply caught the early train from Salisbury, and here I was, old unfaithful Beth, back home and about to take her bath, as usual?

SIMON: Yes, I'd love to. *Little pause.* I thought it was Canterbury.

BETH: It was neither. We spent the night in a hotel in Euston, and the morning in Ned's poky little office at the school, agonizing.

SIMON: Agonizing? Good God, did you really?

BETH: About whether we should give up everything to live together properly.

SIMON: Properly?

BETH: We want, you see, to be husband and wife to each other.

SIMON: Husband *and* wife to each other? Is Ned up to such double duty? And what did you decide?

BETH: Do you care?

SIMON: Yes.

BETH: His wife isn't well. She's been under psychiatric treatment for years. And his daughter is autistic.

SIMON: Oh, I'm sorry. I can quite see why he wants to leave them.

BETH: But I could still leave you.

SIMON: Yes.

BETH: But you don't think I will. Do you?

SIMON: No.

BETH: And why not?

SIMON: Because I hope you'd rather live with me than anybody else, except Ned of course. And I

know you'd rather live with almost anyone than
live alone.

BETH: You think I am that pathetic?

SIMON: I don't think it's pathetic. I'd rather live
with you than anyone else, including Ned. And I
don't want to live alone either.

BETH: But do you want to live at all?

SIMON: What?

BETH: As you hold such a deeply contemptuous
view of human life. That's Ned's diagnosis of you.

SIMON: But the description of my symptoms came
from you, did it?

BETH: He says you're one of those men who only
give permission to little bits of life to get through
to you. He says that while we may envy you your
serenity, we should be revolted by the rot from
which it stems. Your sanity is of the kind that
causes people to go quietly mad around you.

SIMON: What an elegant paraphrase. Tell me, did
you take notes?

BETH: I didn't have to. Every word rang true.

SIMON: But if it's all true, why do you need to keep
referring it back to Ned?

BETH: It's a way of keeping in touch with him. If I
forgot in the middle of a sentence that he's there
and mine, I might begin to scream at you and
claw at you and punch at you.

SIMON: But why should you want to do that?

BETH: Because I hate you.

If, on the other hand, you are reading this scene cold,
without ever having seen it, Beth's first line tells you she
wants information about what Simon knows. Even if you
don't know that Simon is Beth's husband, you have an obvious goal to pursue. Beth's next lines suggest another purpose—to find out *how long* Simon has known. Beth's fifth

line, "You mean you knew I was having an affair because I became boring?" tells you that she has been having an affair, but it is no longer apparent what she is trying to achieve in the scene. In addition, if you are reading the scene cold, you have no real evidence that Beth is telling the truth. At this point, you must improvise a goal for Beth to pursue or you won't know how to react to Simon's next speech. There are at least two more pages of dialogue before Beth says, "We want, you see, to be husband and wife to each other." Until you know what Beth is after, you need something else for her to achieve in the scene. Since you don't know the playwright's intentions, substitute your imagination for his. Your choice of an imaginative goal will bring life to your character.

An interesting goal for Beth would be that she wants Simon to pay more attention to her. She still loves Simon and is just using her affair to make him jealous. She suspects that *he* has been having an affair, and she wants him to give it up. This invention gives you a strong purpose to pursue. It gives a point of view to your lines and provides you with a motive for reacting to whatever your partner does with his lines.

If you are reading for the role of Teach in David Mamet's *American Buffalo* and you are given Teach's scene with Don in the second act, you won't find any clues about what Teach is actually trying to achieve.

TEACH: What time is it?
DON: It's midnight.

Pause.

TEACH: I'm going out there now. I'll need the ad-
    dress. *Teach takes out revolver and begins to load*
    it.

DON: What's that?
TEACH: What?
DON: That.
TEACH: This "gun"?
DON: Yes.
TEACH: What does it look like?
DON: A gun.
TEACH: It *is* a gun.
DON, *rises and crosses to center:* I don't like it.
TEACH: Don't look at it.
DON: I'm serious.
TEACH: So am I.
DON: We don't need a gun, Teach.
TEACH: I pray that we don't, Don.
DON: We don't, tell me why we need a gun.
TEACH: It's not a question do we *need* it . . . *Need*
. . . Only that it makes me comfortable, okay? It
helps me to relax. So, God forbid, something inev-
itable occurs and the choice is (and I'm *saying*
"God forbid") it's either him or us.
DON: Who?
TEACH: The guy. I'm saying God forbid the *guy* (or
somebody) comes in, he's got a knife . . . a cleaver
from one of those magnetic *boards* . . . ?
DON: Yeah?
TEACH: . . . with the two *strips* . . . ?
DON: Yeah?
TEACH: And *whack,* and somebody is bleeding to
death. This is all. Merely as a deterrent. *Pause.* All
the preparation in the world does not mean *shit,*
the path of some crazed lunatic sees you as an
invasion of his personal domain. Guys go nuts,
Don, *you* know this. Public *officials* . . . *Ax* mur-
derers . . . all I'm saying, look out for your own.
DON: I don't like the gun.

> TEACH: It's a personal thing, Don. A personal thing
> of mine. A silly personal thing. I just like to have
> it along. Is this so unreasonable?
> DON: I don't want it.
> TEACH: I'm not going without it.
> DON: Why do you want it?
> TEACH: Protection of me and my partner. Protec-
> tion, deterrence. (We're only going around the
> fucking *corner* for chrissake . . .)
> DON: I don't want it with.
> TEACH: I can't step down on this, Don. I got to have
> it with. The light of things as they are.
> DON: Why?
> TEACH: Because of the way *things* are. *He looks out
> window:* Hold on a second.
> DON: Fletcher?
> TEACH: Cops.
> DON: What are they doing?
> TEACH: Cruising.

Whether you have had a chance to look it over or
are reading this scene cold, you need to know what
Teach is after, or you won't even know how to deliver his first line, "What time is it?" You must decide
what he wants, or there will be no meaning to his
lines with Don while he is cleaning the gun. Obvi-
ously he is planning to do something with the gun,
but what is not clear, and there are no clues to his
relationship with Don either.

An interesting, imaginative purpose to pursue is
that Teach has been assigned to kill Don. He is just
pretending to go out on a robbery. Once he is out
committing the robbery, it will be easier to do away
with Don. This goal brings an immediate nervous
suspense to Teach's first line and his interchange
with Don about the gun. When you get to the point

where Teach has to respond to Don's question "Why do you want it?" Teach's answer, "Protection of me and my partner," will reflect the subterfuge.

Inventing or improvising an imaginative goal to pursue in the reading makes it possible for you to believe in what you are doing without the benefit of rehearsals and discussions with the director. A goal allows you to make your character come alive for your audition audience as if they were watching a finished production. *You cannot make a wrong choice;* at this stage there is no such thing as a "right" or a "wrong" choice. If the director asks you to perform the scene again a different way, you'll know you have convinced him you can act.

10: Showing Your Acting Range

Whoever knows how to improvise, will find it easy to act in a written play.

Andrea Perrucci

Italian playwright

(1651–1704)

When you are auditioning by reading a scene and you have decided what your character wants, *improvise* different ways for him to go about achieving his purpose. Make the choices as interesting as possible to show your acting range. The best method for improvising approaches is to go with ones you enjoy, just as you did with your monologue. These will represent your acting strengths.

It is important that you make an immediate decision about the *nature of your emotional relationship* with the other character in the scene. This means *how you feel* about him, not whether you are lovers or husband and wife or brother and sister.

If you are reading for Beth in the scene from *Otherwise Engaged* and you have decided that her emotional relationship with Simon is that she still loves him, the ways you choose to pursue her goal will be suggested by that feeling. She will be demanding and seductive, sarcastic and vulnerable, angry and funny, and whatever else is appropriate to your goal of getting Simon to carry out her wishes.

If you decide that Beth no longer loves Simon, a different set of means to achieve her goal will spring to mind. If you are reading for Teach in the scene from *American Buffalo,* decide whether he admires, fears, or envies Don. This choice of emotional relationship will immediately bring different approaches to mind and suggest different means of getting Don to go along with Teach's purpose.

To show your acting ability and bring life to your character, you need to vary the approaches you use to achieve your goal, just as you did in your monologue. Since you cannot count on the person you are reading with to give you a reason to change your approach, you must do so on your own. Imagine he has given you a cue, and try something different.

Make an immediate decision about the time, conditions, and place for your scene. Your decision will help focus what you are trying to accomplish by bringing up images for you to work with in the reading. If you decide the scene from *Otherwise Engaged* is taking place in the bedroom at night, there will be a more intimate tone to Beth's dealings with Simon. If you imagine the scene from *American Buffalo* is occurring in a murky basement during a storm, there will be more dramatic suspense in the scene.

If the director stops you and tells you what you are doing is not right for the scene, you'll know he is interested in you. Listen to what he says about your character. Ask for more information. If you ask him questions, you'll remind him that you do not know anything about the play or your role. You will also tell him something about your intelligence and thoroughness, and what you might be like to work with. *Add* what he tells you to your reading. Do not throw out what you have been doing. This is what got him interested in you in the first place.

By making your contribution, using the script as a prop, treating your partner as if you had already rehearsed together, inventing a goal, and showing your acting range, you make the people in your audition audience believe in your imaginary world as if they were watching a finished production. They will care about the character you have created. By taking the risk of inventing and improvising with unfamiliar material, you encourage your prospective employers to identify with *you* as well as with your character. You make them aware of what you might contribute to their production. They will want to have the benefit of your talents.

The
Musical
Audition

When you audition for a musical, you must show your prospective employers that you can act as well as sing. This means that the lyrics of your song must involve your audition audience in what your character is trying to accomplish. To gain their involvement, divide your audition into four parts:

1. *Appearing As Yourself*

2. *Becoming Someone Else*

3. *Performing the Song*

4. *Taking Your Bow*

11: Appearing as Yourself

In all the history of the stage no performer has yet
been able to simulate or make use of a personality
not his own.

William Hooker Gillette

American actor and author

(1855–1937)

When you audition for a musical, you still need to appear
as yourself to give your prospective employers an idea of
what you would be like to work with and to prepare them,
as described in Chapter 1, so that they will be more receptive to what you are about to do.

There will be more people in your musical audition audience than would be at an audition for a play. In addition to
the writers of the book and lyrics, and the composer if the
show is new, you can expect the director, choreographer,
and musical director. Designers and their assistants may
also attend, along with producers, a casting director, and
occasionally even a backer. The tensions and distractions
described in Chapter 1 will be magnified.

Use your entrance to get the attention of the people for
whom you are about to perform, remembering that your
audition begins the moment you appear in their sight line.
Walk slowly over to the accompanist (unless you have
brought your own), and hand him your music.

Your accompanist is the other member of your cast of two for your musical audition. Give him any instructions you have regarding the introduction, tempo, or repetition of choruses, since you have had no chance to rehearse with him. Any cuts or key changes must be easy for the accompanist to read so you don't have to spend too much time talking to him. And the music must be on paper strong enough to stand up on the piano. If possible, your music should be written out in the key you wish to sing it.

Ask the pianist not to start until you nod to him. While you are talking, your audition audience will be aware of you the same way as they were when you entered for your monologue audition. If you look as though you are in a rush to tell your accompanist what to do, you will appear nervous and eager to get your audition over with.

When you have finished instructing the pianist, step into the center of the stage or playing area and introduce yourself with a "hello" or "hi," your name, and your well-planned thought, as discussed in Chapter 1. Taking the time to communicate as yourself at your musical audition not only shows your prospective employers you have the ability to rise above the difficulties of the occasion but also gives you the chance to reach your audition audience with your speaking voice. You will not have this opportunity after they have heard you sing, unless they decide to call you back for a reading.

In musicals, songs usually represent the dramatic highlights of scenes and as such are more emotionally self-contained than monologues. For this reason you will not need to describe the situation confronting your character as you did with your monologue when auditioning for a play. Simply announce the song you will perform and state from what show it comes. The lyrics of the song will bring your prospective employers up to date and involve them immediately in what you are doing.

12: Becoming Someone Else

After appearing as yourself in the first part of your musical audition, you need a brief moment to concentrate before singing your song. You will be singing the sentiments of someone who finds himself in a particular situation. Whether that someone is yourself or a specific character, you need to imagine the situation that precedes the song. Since the music and lyrics will drive the song's emotional content, you will not need as long a moment for concentration as you did for your monologue.

Blocking out the members of your audition audience with whom you have been communicating will once again have a dramatic effect. Close your eyes, stare straight ahead in a freeze, bow your head, or turn your back. This concentration will increase anticipation of your performance, as if the houselights were going down in the theater, and it will tell your prospective employers you have the ability to enter your own world in their presence.

During your moment of concentration, think of two

things: First, imagine the situation confronting your character before the lyric you are about to sing. If you have chosen "Mama, Mama," from *The Most Happy Fella,* imagine that Rosabella has just agreed to marry you. "Hear" her say "Yes!" and visualize her face as she does so. The feeling you get from doing this will propel you into the first line of the song. Second, "hear" the first note or musical phrase of the song you are about to sing.

As soon as you have accomplished this, nod to the pianist to begin. Your signaling will affect your audition audience in the same way an orchestra conductor holding up his baton does. In addition to increasing the excitement, your nod tells your prospective employers you have performed the necessary magic and are prepared to sing as a character in another time and place.

13: Performing the Song

The voice of the actor must alter in its intonations,
according to the qualities that the words express;
from this idea music seems to have taken its birth.

Charles Macklin
Irish actor
(1697–1797)

When you appear in a musical, you are performing a role, just as you would in a play. By using your ability to sing and dance, you enhance your character's ability to express himself within the context of the musical's story.

In your audition, you need to show the power and beauty of your voice, and you need to demonstrate that you can use your voice to bring your character to life. To select the best songs for these purposes, look at each song without the music, as if it were a monologue. Decide whether the content of the lyric represents the kind of character that will convey your acting strengths.

The fact that your character will be singing rather than speaking should not change your method of selecting audition material. Be sure that the character you portray is the kind of role you enjoy doing.

You will normally have two opportunities to sing, an up-tempo song and a ballad. This means you can bring two kinds of characters to life. Come prepared with at least six songs in case more than two are asked for. Choose songs that are as different as possible in emotional content to show your acting range. Your audition audience will assume that you can play all the roles in between.

Remember that if you succeed in involving your prospective employers in the emotional life of the character you portray, they will want you for their production. The people you are auditioning for want to present the best talent available. If they can't find an appropriate part for you, they may write one in, or they may remember you for their next production.

Do not alter one of your chosen and rehearsed audition songs for a character you think you might be right for in a particular show. If you are a thirty-year-old soprano who expresses herself best with a romantic ballad, and the part you want calls for a soprano aged twenty-five to forty-five who can play a strong and blustery character, *do not* try to put those qualities into your song.

After your audition audience has identified with the romantic character you've brought to life, the director may ask you to perform the song differently, or he may ask you for another song that brings out the strong and blustery side of your acting range. He may try to get you to develop these qualities when you read a scene from the show. That's his job. The important thing in your audition is to captivate your prospective employers with your chosen song. That is the only way they will become interested in *you*.

The lyrics of your song must involve your audition audience in what your character is trying to accomplish in the same manner that a dramatic monologue would. In other words, the lyrics must explain who is saying what to whom and why. The answers to these questions are usually found in the verse section of a song, which sets up the more general chorus. Therefore, begin with the verse. In situations in which you are limited to sixteen bars, begin with the verse, even if doing so means you won't reach the part of the chorus that shows off your best notes. If you involve your listeners in the emotional content of your song, you may be allowed to continue.

If the director stops you, treat it as the planned ending for your performance, as you would if your monologue were interrupted. This becomes another opportunity to show your prospective employers your adaptability. Assume you were stopped because the director likes you. Your enthusiasm and good humor may be just the spark needed to produce a callback.

Pick the song you enjoy doing most for the first number in your musical audition. If you are auditioning for a musical with a familiar operatic aria, do it in English so the audition audience can understand the text as part of a dramatic scene.

Whether your song is directed to a particular person or represents a conversation your character is having with himself, the song is addressed to someone. Establish the location of the imaginary person who is listening, just as you would for a dramatic monologue. Once again, never use a member of your audition audience for your imaginary partner. He will become an unwilling participant in your act and be unable to enter your imaginary world as a member of an audience.

In your musical audition, you will not have the opportunity to stop and react to your imaginary partner as you would with a monologue. The music itself, with its rests and pauses, will dictate where you need to react. Write out the lyrics of your song as if it were a monologue. Fill in the places where there are rests, pauses, and sustained notes with imaginary dialogue for yourself or your imaginary partner. The dialogue should be related to what you hope to accomplish with your song. When you are not singing, you can react to this imaginary dialogue as you would to your imaginary partner with a monologue. Vary the beats to show your acting range, and write in directions for yourself whenever you wish to change what you are doing.

If you treat your song as a monologue that is part of a scene, your breathing and phrasing will automatically follow the thoughts expressed, as if you were speaking them to another character. Your audition audience will identify with what your character wants, as if they were watching a scene from a play. Do not "stage" your audition song. Remain in position, and allow the lyrics to express your intent. In other words, pour your emotion into the song itself instead of "being emotional" as you sing.

At the end of your song, or after the sixteen or thirty-two bars you have selected to perform, go into a freeze, just as you would at the end of a dramatic monologue. Remain "in character," thinking of the sentiments you've just expressed for a full three seconds before relaxing and bowing with your thank-you.

Not letting your audition audience know exactly when you are about to return to yourself allows them time to realize that they entered the imaginary world of the character you portrayed in your song. That realization will tell them you are capable of performing as a singing actor in a musical.

14: Taking Your Bow

Assume a virtue if you have it not.

William Shakespeare (1564–1616),

Hamlet, III. iv. 160

Whether you are an actor who sings, a singer who acts, or a dancer who does both, you need to show your audition audience that you know what it means to *perform* in a musical. Use your bow and thank-you at the end of your audition to accomplish this. If you used a short song you arranged, or even if you only sang sixteen bars, you need an ending to your audition show. When you take your bow, "hear" the applause that acknowledges your successful performance. Smile when you say "thank you," as if you were saying "you're welcome." Your satisfaction with your success will communicate itself to your prospective employers the same way as the thoughts you expressed in your song did. You will help them decide to ask you to sing another song, to have you read a scene, or to call you back. You will make them want to applaud your performance.

IV

The
Interview

When you are interviewed by a director, producer, author, casting director, agent, or representative of a regional or repertory theater, there is no set format for what will take place. To show you can act, you need a script. Prepare a monologue with yourself as the central character. The script and the way you perform it must make your interviewer care about you and what you want to achieve. It must also give you a chance to show your acting strengths.

15: What Your Interviewer Really Wants to Know

When you are interviewed, your prospective employer is deciding whether he should take the time to arrange a formal audition for you. He will do this only if he sees something in the interview that makes him want you for his production. He really wants to know if you can act, but he won't say so. As an alternative, he will ask you questions like "What have you done lately?" or "Can you tell me something about yourself?"

Instead of reciting your résumé, which he already has in front of him, show him you can act. Since you cannot do this without a script, write one in advance. Make yourself the central character so you can go into your prepared material without having to stop and ask him if he wants to hear something.

Before beginning your personal monologue, relax your interviewer. Make him feel like the audience in a theater when the houselights go down. Make him look forward to getting to know you. Accomplish this by taking an interest in him and asking questions.

If your interviewer is the producer or director of the show you hope to be hired for, ask him to tell you something about the production. If he is a casting director, ask him how he got the job and whether he finds it interesting. If he is an agent, ask him whom he represents. If he runs a regional or repertory theater, ask him something specific about the company, such as how long it has been in existence or where it gets its funding. By making your interviewer the focus of attention, you demonstrate confidence in yourself and show him you will be an active participant. This means he won't have to work so hard to draw things out of you. It also indicates that you are not desperate for the job and can afford to be interested in something other than yourself.

The person who is interviewing you has a job to do. If he is a director or author or producer, he needs to find the best available actors for his upcoming show. If he runs a regional theater, he wants the best talent in his company to give it the kind of reputation that will bring in other talent, the best possible reviews, and the funding that will ensure the theater's survival. If he is a casting director or an agent, he needs to find exciting new actors to represent. By helping him get to know you, you assist him in fulfilling his task.

Once your interviewer knows you will not be waiting for him to initiate everything, he will relax and become receptive to what you are doing.

16: Your Personal Monologue

A play is material for acting. It may be far more, but
it must be that to begin with.

Harley Granville-Barker

English actor and dramatist

(1877–1946)

The script for your personal monologue should come from your life experience and must allow you to show your acting strengths. Make it conform to the same principles as the monologue you choose for your formal audition. The central character is yourself, the most interesting person you know. This is a role you should enjoy playing. The script must deal with a conflict you need to resolve over something that is important to you. This content allows your interviewer to identify with what you are trying to achieve.

Make a list of your acting strengths. If you are not sure what they are, write down the kinds of characters you would enjoy playing. Then write a description of yourself in the third person, as if you were a character in a novel. Include your acting strengths or the characteristics of the roles you would enjoy, or both. Include characteristics from roles you would enjoy *even if they are not typical of you personally.* Some actors are at their best when playing themselves, some are better at playing other people.

If your acting strengths lie in roles in which the character is tough, cynical, and sexy, you might write

Jane was a California native, just on the wrong side of forty, childless, with two broken marriages. She was tough-guy cynical and sexy. It was her blunt edge, her inability to suppress whatever came into her head, that made her appear somewhat coarse. But the shock value of her remarks, salted with foul language, gave her an entrée into the male world of stock hype, where she was a trusted member of the fraternity.

This is actually the description of a character from a novel by Warren Adler.

If you would enjoy playing characters who are experienced, knowledgeable, and exotic, write

Jane was a California native, just on the wrong side of forty, childless, with two broken marriages. She exuded experience and wisdom, and conveyed a sense that she had somehow managed to survive psychic plagues, mysterious sexual wars, failed love affairs, an abused childhood, and an economic bashing. The fact was, she was an exotic bird.

After you have written this description, write a scene with dialogue in which you have a chance to display these qualities. The scene can be one that actually occurred, or you can create your own. Then construct your personal monologue by incorporating the dialogue you wrote for yourself, leaving out the lines of the other characters.

If your acting strengths are character roles, you might write

Lately I have been wondering why I want to be in this business. I guess it started when I was a kid. I was an only child, and whenever I played alone, I would pretend I was a famous actress. I acted out everything. I knew the whole script of *The Wizard of Oz:*

"Who killed my sister? Who killed the witch of the East? Was it you?"
"No. It was an accident. I didn't mean to kill anybody."
"Well, my little pretty, I can cause accidents, too."
"Oh, rubbish. You have no power here. Begone—before somebody drops a house on you."
"Very well. I'll bide my time. But just try to stay out of my way. Just try. I'll get you, my pretty. And your little dog, too. Ahhh, ha, ha, ha!"

By beginning with "Lately I have been wondering why...," you prepare yourself in advance for the interviewer's questions—"What have you done lately?" or "What can you tell me about yourself?"—and then you can go into your personal monologue as if it were a response to his question. By portraying characters at the beginning of your monologue, you announce to your interviewer that you will be performing for him after all, but in the context of the story you are telling, not in a way that requires his response. This format allows him to relax and experience what you are doing as if he were part of an audience in a theater. Then you can develop your theme:

> Whatever I pretended, I was always very famous and I was always helping people. In school I was quiet and clumsy and scared. Then I got my big chance: The girl who was playing Pinocchio in our annual show got sick, and I took over. That was it for me.
> I've been performing ever since. I recall my whole life in terms of what show I was doing and where. I'm still basically a shy person, and I love being able to reach people and make them care and feel things by my being another character. The only problem is lately the parts and plays seem to be deteriorating.

You can finish by asking, "Is this what has happened to the theater, or have I been seeing the wrong people?"

When you end your personal monologue with "The only problem is lately . . . ," you are closing before resolving your conflict, just as you did in the monologue audition (see page 16). When you ask for advice, you invite your interviewer's participation in resolving your conflict, as if you had been having a conversation with him. This allows him to continue a dialogue with you.

Your personal monologue gives you the opportunity to play an array of characters within the context of the story you are telling about yourself. When you speak as Dorothy and the Wicked Witch of the West, you display your talent for character roles. When you describe yourself as someone who loves "to reach people and make them care and feel things," you present a motive for wanting to act that your interviewer can identify with.

When you are preparing your personal monologue, you don't have to make actual dialogue part of your script. You can act the roles of the characters at the same time you describe them. Here's an example:

As a kid I never knew what I wanted to be. Maybe a better way to put it is that I wanted to be everything. I remember when I met a glamorous businesswoman, I decided right then and there I wanted to be a corporate executive like her. She was wearing the most gorgeous full-length fur coat I had ever seen. Her suit was impeccably tailored. Her posture was erect and perfect. She looked so self-assured. Then I met a judge. She had an air of always being in control. She exuded power. She was the essence of judiciousness and looked like she always knew right from wrong. She had an answer for everything. She was crisp, clean, and intellectual. I wanted to be her. Then there was a television talk-show host who was incredibly articulate. He could be very sharp-tongued and biting. He had an opinion on everything. He put people down so subtly they thought they were being complimented. I wanted to be able to do that. I decided to become an actress so I could be all of these people.

Here the descriptions of the corporate executive, judge, and TV talk-show host serve as your script for becoming those characters. As you describe them, take on their voices, facial expressions, and body positions. The effect is even more magical without dialogue, as if acting is such an integral part of you that it is impossible for you to talk about someone without immediately becoming that person.

When you are appearing in a play, your qualities are blended with those of the character the author has created. The resulting combination of you and that character is what the audience meets and identifies with. Even though you know in advance every word you will speak, where you will stand, when you will move, and what you will look like, your unique personality affects everything you do. The author's words are the foundation on which you build a living character.

This is also true in your interview. By writing a scripted monologue in advance, with yourself as the central character, you give yourself the chance to play a role with which your interviewer can identify. By using material such as the moment you first knew you wanted to act, why you love acting, a detailed description of your last audition, or any scene from life that you were part of and had meaning for you, you bring to life the truest and most "actable" part of yourself. Doing this will make your interviewer want to arrange a formal audition for you to see if he can use your talents, and he will take a personal interest in the result to see if he can help write a happy ending to your story.

V

Rehearsing
Your
Audition

17: Practicing with a Group

Fellow actors and audiences are the only means by
which an actor may gauge the effect of his acting.

John Gielgud
English actor
(1904–)

The technique for auditioning presented in the first sixteen chapters of this book must be put into practice to be fully understood. As with any technique, it should be absorbed to the point where it becomes second nature.

Before you begin auditioning for prospective employers, rehearse each of the four situations you will encounter. Form a group with several of your fellow actors to serve as your audition audience. Assign each member a role, as the author, director, or producer of the play or musical for which you are holding auditions. This is an important part of learning the technique. By imagining you are a prospective employer, you feel what it is like to be on the other side of the audition footlights. You discover and pinpoint the exact moment when one of your colleagues makes you experience the magic click and makes you feel like the audience in a theater. This helps you when it is your turn to audition.

Use your group to try out and edit the original material you need for the appearance as yourself and for your personal monologue. When you rehearse the reading, have a member of the group read with you while the others act as your audition audience.

Select a member of the group to be the director in charge. Begin by working on the audition for which you choose your own monologue. Each time you audition one of your fellow actors, imagine you have never seen him before so you can form an objective opinion of his presentation. As each actor auditions, write down the answers to these five questions:

1. What is your opinion of the actor's acting ability?

2. Could you get any impression of the actor's ability to sustain a role, beyond what he did with his monologue?

3. Did you get a sense of the actor's personality and what he might be like to work with? If so, what was your impression?

4. Do you think the actor picked the best role to show off his talents?

5. If you do not think the actor chose the best material to represent himself, what type of role or material would you like to see this actor try?

When each actor finishes his audition, compare your answers to these five questions under the guidance of the director and in the presence of your fellow actor. This is the process the people you audition for go through at the end of a day of auditioning. The only difference is that you are not present to hear it. The conclusions you come to will affect the actor's choice of material and will give him an idea of the kind of impression he is making.

Approximate the conditions of an audition: Have the actor who is appearing in front of the group wait out of sight until he is called. Have a member of the group act as stage manager and call out "Number 678!" When the actor enters, have the stage manager introduce him. During the audition, have the group write down their answers to the five questions, pass the actor's résumé around, and do anything else they feel appropriate. Then have the director thank the actor at the end of his audition, and have the actor exit.

Have each actor present two contrasting monologues in his first audition for the group. They can be a combination of comic and serious, or classic and contemporary. The actor should describe both monologues during the appearance as himself before he takes a moment to become someone else.

The second time a member of the group auditions, the director should stop him in the middle of his monologue with a "thank you very much!" to see how he handles it. Everyone should be given a chance to experience being interrupted in this manner.

Evaluate the four parts of each actor's audition: appearing as yourself, becoming someone else, performing the monologue, and taking your bow. *Pinpoint the exact moment you decided you liked the actor enough to call him back for a reading,* if such a moment occurred. What was it that captured your interest? Was there a moment when you experienced the magic click and started to feel like a member of an audience in a theater watching a performance? Were you *involved* with the actor when he appeared as himself so that you cared what happened to him? Did you have the same involvement with each of the characters the actor portrayed in his monologues? When and how was the actor able to capture your involvement?

Each time you audition, try out a different original thought during the appearance as yourself, until you arrive at the one with which you feel the most comfortable. If you cannot think of anything to say during the appearance as yourself, improvise whatever comes to mind. Express your feelings about auditioning, with humor if possible. Improvising is the best way to find the most effective material since it comes from your innermost self. Remember that your purpose is to show your prospective employers you have the capability to rise above the adverse circumstances of the audition.

If you are auditioning for the group and you have no monologues committed to memory, use one from the numerous collections sold in drama bookstores. Hold the book in your hand, and grab sentences with your eyes as described on pages 29–30. When the group evaluates your material, decide whether to continue working on the monologues you picked or try new ones. In subsequent meetings, distribute copies of each monologue you use so your fellow actors can suggest editing to make your monologue more effective.

As members of the group get to know you, they can help you with your choice of monologues. They will know if your unique personality traits are being used in the roles with which you audition. They will know if your sense of humor is evident only offstage. They will be able to tell you if your material is overpowering your audition, and if you need some new subjects besides sex and murder.

When you are listening to a monologue by one of your fellow actors, ask yourself who is saying what to whom and why? Are you spending your time trying to figure out what is happening, or can you immediately identify with what the character is seeking to achieve? Should the description of the situation confronting the character be changed so it involves you more immediately in the action?

Evaluate the physical appearance and movements of the actor auditioning. Does his posture and body language support what he is trying to achieve as the character? Does each suggest confidence and self-assurance when he appears as himself? Does he seem relaxed and in control of the stage when he enters and exits? Does he use his voice effectively?

Does he have sufficient variety in the time, volume, pitch, and energy of his line readings?

Is the actor using the playing area effectively? Is he making the proper choice for center stage? Is he observing the principle of "less is more" with minimal movement? Is he picking the right point of focus for his imaginary partner so that each member of the audition audience feels involved in what he is doing?

Use your group to practice what to do if you forget your lines in the middle of your audition. If you are far enough into your piece, freeze for a full three seconds and then bow and say your thank-you. Instead of appearing as if you have made a mistake and lost your way, it will seem like the place you planned to end the monologue. The spontaneity of the moment will be even greater in its effect than if you had planned it, and you will leave your audition audience in the kind of suspense that will make them want to hear more. If you go up on your lines at the beginning of your monologue, when it is too early for the "accidentally planned" ending, announce that you will be starting the speech again. Do not apologize, and do not ask for permission to begin again. Starting over will give you another chance to impress your prospective employers with your ability to shift back and forth from yourself to the character, and it will also tell them you are determined to live up to your potential in a professional way.

Plan drills in which your stage manager stops you after exactly two minutes. This method will help you edit your monologues so they can be effective in that time period. It will also prepare you for auditions when that is all the time you will be given.

Wear the clothes you plan to use for auditions so your fellow actors can evaluate them.

Pay special attention to the first impression each actor makes when he begins his audition, speaking as himself. Is he confident? Is he enjoying himself? Does he appear to have stage presence?

When you rehearse the reading, use scenes from plays you have never seen before. Have one member of the group serve as your partner while the rest act as the audition audience. Once again, approximate the conditions of the audition. Ask the director of the group for permission to look over the material. When he turns you down, enjoy the freedom of improvising and becoming the playwright.

Have the director stop both you and your partner whenever either of you looks at the script while speaking or listening. The more you practice, the more words you will be able to grab in a glance when you use the script as a prop.

As you work with your partner, practice improvising goals with maximum use of your imagination to give yourself more to work with. Make the ways your character achieves what he wants as varied as possible. In discussion with your group after the reading, you will discover whether you held their attention. You will also find out whether they were sufficiently involved to care what happened to your character.

Practice doing a reading when you have a few minutes to look over the scene, and become accustomed to inventing a goal for your character in these circumstances. Pay attention to your partner, and make sure you are not both doing the same thing at the same time. Acting in unison reduces the conflict and drama of what is taking place. Ask your group to tell you if you kept the conflict alive, or if the reading became boring.

Rehearse your reading with a member of the group who behaves as a bored stage manager rather than another actor auditioning. Treat him as if he were an actor you had already rehearsed with. Learn to adapt the ways you pursue your goal to whatever he is doing or expressing.

Practice working with your director as if you already had the job and were rehearsing the play with him. When he tells you more about your character and the scene you are reading, ask intelligent questions that show your desire to be thorough. Add to your character the dimensions or colors he suggests, without throwing away what you have already achieved, remembering he would not be telling you anything if you had not captured his interest.

Have the director of your group stop you at different times in each reading with a Thank-you. Assume he stopped you because he liked what he saw. Rather than acting surprised or annoyed, say "Thank you" to him as if you were taking a curtain call. Remember that *your* attitude toward your work affects your audition audience. Practice infecting others with enthusiasm for what you have accomplished.

When you are observing your fellow actors reading, decide whether they are *making things happen.* Are they making contact with each other? Are they reacting to each other? Are they acting as if they have already rehearsed with their partner, so they are free to react spontaneously in each moment no matter what their partner is or is not doing?

Rehearse your musical audition for the group with a hired accompanist. Practice your entrance by handing him your music, giving him instructions, and then taking your chosen position in front of the group. Try out different songs, and practice the four parts to your audition. Ask for feedback from your colleagues. Switch roles and try to imagine you've never heard the member of your group sing before. Did he involve you in the character he portrayed in his song? Ask him to perform the song with different musical dynamics. Ask him to perform it with a different dramatic intention. Request another song that sets a different mood.

Practice following up your song with a contrasting monologue. If your song is an up-tempo number, do a serious dramatic monologue. Some audition situations call for just this kind of combination.

Ask the member of your group who is auditioning to do

a reading of a scene. Practice going into your reading technique with a member of the group right after you have auditioned with your song.

In all these situations, keep the atmosphere of an audition, paying special attention to what happens between musical numbers, and between songs and monologues or scenes. Remember, it is the overall impression of what you would be like to work with, combined with your enthusiasm and talent, which will ultimately convince your prospective employers to put you in their show.

Work on your personal monologue for the interview, using your group as the interviewer. Improvise answers to why, when, and how you decided to become an actor. Act out recent audition experiences, playing the roles of some of the people for whom you auditioned. This is the best way to find material that will work for you.

Practice doing an interview on the stage with a member of the group acting as the interviewer and with the rest of your fellow actors observing. Go into your prepared material after the interviewer has asked you to tell him something about yourself or has said, "What have you done lately?"

Change roles with your partner, becoming the interviewer yourself. Interrupt the actor you are interviewing at different points during his monologue with "What's the problem?" and "How does this concern me?" giving him practice in finding a way to get back into his text. Act the role of a tired or bored interviewer to give your partner the chance to see if he can arouse your interest. Stare at him to see if he can find a way to get into his prepared material under scrutiny.

Rehearse walking into an office by setting up an office situation with a chair and a desk in full view of the group that is acting as observers. Practice walking to the side of the person rather than standing in front of him, so he doesn't feel he is being confronted. Rehearse asking for advice, as if it were a producer's office or the reception area of a regional theater company. Practice going into your personal monologue. Reverse roles with your partner, becoming the disinterested person behind the desk.

When you evaluate these improvised performances, express yourself as the character you played before the members of the group give their opinions. If you were the busy director of a regional theater sitting behind the desk, did the actor without an appointment get your attention without antagonizing you? Did he make you root for him and involve you in his story with his personal monologue? Did he make you want to arrange an audition for him?

Working with a group of your fellow actors allows you to rehearse your audition effectively. Your colleagues can use their acting talent to play the roles of the people for whom you will be auditioning. And as you do the same for them, you will gain insight into what it's like to be a prospective employer.

VI

Getting
Your
Audition

18: Reading the Trades

When you are ready to start auditioning, read the trade papers. Look in *Back Stage, Variety, Show Business, Ross Reports,* and everything else you can get your hands on. Audition for anyone who will see you. *Don't bypass an audition because the type they are looking for doesn't sound like you.* Audition for old men and old ladies, people who are fat or thin, and different ethnic types. Acting means becoming someone else. Don't underestimate your own ability. Remember, *your prospective employers don't know what they are looking for.* If they did, they would have called "the right actor" and hired him. Until someone shows up and reads the dialogue, the character is just words printed on a page.

Don't be misled by character descriptions. People holding auditions have to put a description in the papers to get actors to show up. If you don't fit the character description they came up with but still give an interesting reading, your acting talent will appear all the more impressive. If the author, director, and producer don't change their minds and give you the part, they may consider you for another role. The author might decide to write in a part for you. The director may remember you when he is casting his next show. Keep showing up at auditions. Be persistent.

If you audition for a regional theater or repertory group, surprise your prospective employers by making your first choice a character whose physical appearance differs from your own. Everyone will assume you can act people you resemble. Versatility is what they are looking for.

Use the trade papers to find opportunities for interviews, readings, and general auditions. If an interview turns into an opportunity to do a monologue or a reading, you can switch gears on the spot, since you have the expertise for all three.

19: Getting Appointments

Ask friends and relatives who they know in the world of show business. Casting directors, agents, television and film executives, and anyone working in theater can be of help, provided you get to see them. See anyone you can. Don't stop to consider whether someone in the film industry can get you a role on the stage. Maybe he knows someone in theater, if that is your favorite area of work. On the other hand, he might think you are right for a part in a movie. Would this damage your theatrical career?

If a friend knows someone in the business but does not want to arrange an appointment, ask for the name and telephone number of his contact and permission to mention your friend's name. If your friend doesn't want his name mentioned, be grateful for his help and try to arrange the appointment without mentioning your friend's name.

Do not try to sell yourself over the telephone. The magic of theater happens between actor and audience. Tell the person you are speaking to you need some advice, and ask for an appointment at his convenience. Successful and busy people usually enjoy giving advice.

When you get to see someone through your own efforts or with a friend's help, treat your appointment as an interview, and use your personal monologue to show your acting ability.

20: Walking In

Create opportunities for yourself by walking into offices and spending time with the people who inhabit them. Ask questions in person in the offices of producers, directors, agents, casting directors, and repertory theaters. (The Theatre Communications Group, or TCG, publishes a book that lists regional and repertory theaters around the country. It details the kinds of plays each group produces and gives the names of the business manager and artistic director of each company.)

While you're in an office, valuable information may come your way, or someone may see you and invite you to audition. While you are talking with the receptionist for a repertory theater, the director of the next production may walk by and see and hear you. Maybe the person at the receptionist's desk *is* the director of the next production, going through the company files to find a replacement for a cast member who has just been lost to a television series.

Acting is the art of persuasion. The actor persuades the

audience by first persuading himself to believe in what he is doing. To get an audition, you need to persuade someone to take a look at the "product" you are "selling," which is yourself. Producers, authors, directors, agents, casting directors, film and television company executives, and officers of regional and repertory theater companies are all, in some sense, salespeople themselves. Selling is part of life in show business, as it is in any business. That is how productions get put together. Salespeople are susceptible to other salespeople. Unless there is a "keep out" sign with Dobermans standing guard, a door exists to be opened. Waiting on the other side is another salesperson like yourself.

21: Preparing Your Résumé

A résumé is a calling card and conversation piece, but it can't get you a job on its own. Most résumés end up in files or trash baskets. If your photo is stunning, you might get a response by mailing it out for work in film or television, but you would be better off arranging live auditions. Leave your photo/résumé behind after an interview or after you have met someone by walking into an office.

Your photograph should resemble your present age, hairstyle, and all other physical characteristics. You should not be posed in it as if the photographer told you to smile or look mysterious. If you are, modeling will seem to be your main profession. Your photograph will help you look like an actor if you are immersed in a role when it is taken. To achieve this, be photographed while you are doing one of your audition monologues.

If you are applying for a job in theater, list your theatrical credits first, followed by those for film and television. Theater people are sensitive about losing talent to the film and television industries and may take it personally if you tell them film is your first love. If you can afford only one résumé, use the one that begins with your theatrical credits. Film and television people respect actors with a theatrical background.

The most important function of your résumé is to support the opinion of someone who has taken an interest in you. When you audition, your résumé is slipped under the director's nose while you are making your entrance. The photograph is turned away from him since he has you to look at. If something about you interests the director, he will glance down at the text while you are performing. He wants to be reassured about your experience.

The first thing he'll notice is bulk. The page should not be overcrowded but should reflect that you have been busy. If your audition continues to interest him, the director will look for classic roles, since they indicate the depth of your theatrical background. These should be listed first among your theatrical credits. Small roles performed in New York should be listed ahead of large roles performed elsewhere. If you were directed by or appeared in a show with a well-known theater personality, include his or her name. The director you are auditioning for may want to ask that person for a reference.

Never put anything in your résumé that isn't true. What may seem, in a moment of poetic license, to be harmless padding can come back to haunt you and might in fact *cost* you a job rather than *get* you one. If you falsely claim, for example, to have performed your favorite role at an obscure summer stock theater in Maine several seasons ago you might find that the owner of that playhouse is in your audition audience. He will not be amused.

If you do not have enough credits to fill up a résumé, list what you have done under the heading "Representative Roles." This allows you to put down parts you performed in college, school, camp, and so on. Even roles you have studied or wish to perform can be listed under this heading.

If the director asks you where you have performed one of them, it means he is interested enough to find out more about your background. When you tell him you have never performed the role in a professional production, he may become curious about what you do with it. If a director has become interested in your talent at an audition, he may want to be the one to discover you. Your lack of experience may work in your favor. This is also true if you have never performed in New York. Everyone has to start somewhere, and directors, authors, and producers like to present talent that has never been seen before.

Don't rush out and have a new résumé printed every time you get a job. Penciling in your most recent credits indicates that you are more interested in working than in keeping your résumé up to date.

A résumé cannot get you a job, but it can help after you have had a successful audition.

VII

After a Successful Audition

22: Callbacks

If you are called back to audition again, act as though you were auditioning for the first time. Wear the same clothes and hairstyle and perform the same monologue or song you used for your first audition.

You are being called back because something about what you did and the way you did it convinced your prospective employers you can act. You accomplished the magic click and drew the people in your audition audience into your imaginary world. Now they want to see if you can repeat the magic. If you can, they will want to see if you can bring the same magic to one of the roles in their upcoming production.

If you are auditioning for a play, the director may ask you for a monologue that brings out a different side of your acting range, *but only after he has seen you repeat what you already did.* He wants to be convinced it was not just an accident. Instead of another monologue, he may ask you to read a scene from the play, in which case you can go into your reading technique.

Do not perform a monologue from the play you are auditioning for, even if you are familiar with the play and the role you want—unless, of course, the director specifically asks you to do so. Your prospective employers have their own ideas about how the roles should be performed. Wait until you have *re*captured their interest with a repeat performance of your monologue. You have a better chance of getting advice and information about the character if you are asked to read a scene. By volunteering a monologue from the play, you may be shutting off that possibility.

If you are called back for a musical, perform the song or songs you used at your first audition. Be prepared with others in case the director wants to see a different side of your musical acting repertoire. Do not change the way you performed the songs at your first audition unless the director specifically asks you to. Remember, it was your original performance that interested him in the first place.

Do not perform a song from the musical you are auditioning for, even if you are familiar with the show and think you know what part suits you best. The director may have you in mind for something else. Give him time to get to know you, and wait for him to tell you what he's thinking. Make the character in your chosen song come to life, and be prepared with songs from the show in case the director asks for them after you have gained his interest.

Do not perform another song by the composer of the musical for which you are auditioning. Doing so will look as if you are trying to ingratiate yourself and will put you in competition with the composer's ideal rendition of his creation.

If you are auditioning to replace someone in a musical, be prepared with your usual audition songs, and do them first. Have the director get to know your talent on your own terms. Then be prepared to perform songs from the show when asked to do so. If you have seen the production of the musical for which you are auditioning, incorporate some of the simpler aspects of the staging into your performance.

Remember that your callback is an even more in-depth exploration of what it would be like to work with you. Some of the things the director asks you to do may simply be a way of finding out if you can take direction. Be willing to experiment with new approaches to your songs or monologues if asked to do so. Ask the director for more information on anything that is not clear to you. He will welcome your desire to be thorough and professional in your work.

23: If You Are an Established Performer

If you are an established performer or someone the director knows and has already worked with, do not take offense at being asked to audition. Think of the audition as an exciting opportunity to explore sides of your acting range that even you may not be aware of. Perhaps you and your public are only familiar with one aspect of your theatrical personality. You are being asked to audition because the director believes there are some other colors to develop. Give him the chance to see whether he can help bring them out.

Whether the new approach is to a monologue or a song or a part you are reading for, remain open to things you never thought you were capable of. Perhaps you have grown and changed since the last time you worked with the director. Perhaps *he* has grown and changed. Let the magic of theater catch up with both of you and show you new possibilities. The result might be rewarding.

Summary

The audition technique that has been presented in this book can be learned and practiced. With this technique you can perform for your prospective employers as if they were an audience in a theater; you will be able to entice your audition audience into your imaginary world.

When you appear alone with a monologue of your choice, appearing as yourself, becoming someone else, performing the monologue, and taking your bow, are all part of a complete performance that is written, directed, and rehearsed in advance. Using an imaginary partner allows you to plan and rehearse your monologue to show your acting strengths.

When you read a scene with another person, the technique enables you to give life to your character and involve your audition audience in the face of unknown quantities. You accomplish this by making your contribution, using the script as a prop, treating your partner as if you had already rehearsed together, inventing a goal, and showing your acting range.

When you audition for a musical, appearing as yourself, becoming someone else, performing the song, and taking your bow are once again part of a complete performance which is planned and rehearsed in advance. By treating the text of the song as if it were part of a scene, you bring your character to life as if you were appearing in a play.

When you are interviewed, understanding what your interviewer really wants to know allows you to relax him and make him receptive to what you are about to do, and the use of your personal monologue gives you the opportunity to show your acting strengths as if you were appearing at a formal audition.

In each of the four audition situations, the technique gives you the ability to involve your prospective employers in what you are trying to achieve so they will root for your success.

Whether you are a beginner or an established actor, auditioning will be with you for the rest of your career. With this technique, you can enjoy auditioning as much as you enjoy acting.

Think of your life as a play. You are the central character. An actor in a play knows more than the character he is portraying, since he knows what will happen at the end of the drama. If you could see into your future, you might discover that the occasions when you explored new opportunities were some of the most interesting in your life.

If you enjoy your audition, others will, too.

Appendix: Where to Find Monologues, Songs, and Practice Scenes

Here are some of the best places to buy monologue collections, sheet music, and scene books to practice auditioning:

BOOKSTORES—NEW YORK CITY

Actor's Heritage
262 West Forty-fourth Street
New York, NY 10036
(212) 944-7490

Applause Theatre Books
211 West Seventy-first Street
New York, NY 10023
(212) 496-7511

Coliseum Books
1771 Broadway
New York, NY 10019
(212) 757-8381

Drama Book Shop
723 Seventh Avenue
New York, NY 10019
(212) 944-0595

Theatre Arts Bookstore
405 West Forty-second Street
New York, NY 10036
(212) 564-0402

Theatrebooks
1600 Broadway
Room 1009
New York, NY 10019
(212) 757-2834

BOOKSTORES—LOS ANGELES

Larry Edmunds Bookshop
6658 Hollywood Boulevard
Hollywood, CA 90028
(213) 463-3273

Larry Edmunds Bookshop
11969 Ventura Boulevard
Studio City, CA 91604
(818) 508-7511

Samuel French
7623 Sunset Boulevard
Los Angeles, CA 90046
(213) 876-0570

Samuel French
11963 Ventura Boulevard
Studio City, CA 91604
(818) 762-0535

BOOKSTORES—LONDON

Dillons, the Bookstore
1 Malet Street
London WC1E 7JB
071-636-1577

W & G Foyle Ltd.
113–119 Charing Cross Road
London WC2H OEB
071-437-5660

Samuel French, Ltd.
52 Fitzroy Street
London W1P 6JR
071-387-9373

Offstage Theatre and Cinema Bookshop
37 Chalk Farm Road
London NW1 8AJ
071-485-4996

SHEET MUSIC STORES—NEW YORK CITY

Colony Music
1619 Broadway
New York, NY 10019
(212) 265-2050
Large selection of current in-print sheet music and some
out-of-print sheets; selection of phonograph records, both
in print and out of print.

Music Exchange
151 West Forty-sixth Street
New York, NY 10036
(212) 354-5858
Large selection of out-of-print sheet music.

SHEET MUSIC STORES—LONDON

Chappel of Bond Street
50 Bond Street
London W1Y 9HA
071-491-2777

ABOUT THE AUTHOR

David Black was born and educated in New York City. As an undergraduate at Harvard College, he performed leading roles in operettas, and after graduation he pursued an operatic career in Europe. After several years on Wall Street as an award-winning salesman, he began a career as a Broadway producer. He has produced eighteen shows, winning Tony Awards and presenting some of the theater's brightest stars. In 1968 he was invited to produce the Presidential Inaugural Gala. Mr. Black has directed in New York and London and has lectured and given master classes on auditioning. His popular course "The Magic of Theatre" is in its fourth semester at The New School. Mr. Black complements his teaching with a career as a prolific artist.